MW01101522

The Bible in a Nutshell

BY REVEREND
DALE J. PRITCHARD

The Bible in a Nutshell

BY REVEREND
DALE J. PRITCHARD

Jain Publishing Company
Fremont, California

Pritchard, Dale J., 1960-
    The Bible in a nutshell / by Dale J. Pritchard.
        p   cm.
    ISBN 0-87573-029-9
    I. Bible--Outlines, syllabi, etc.   I.Title.
BS418.P75 1994
220'.02'02--dc20   94--11993
                                                           CIP

Printed in Hong Kong

*I dedicate this book
to my mother—
who made sure that religious values
were a part of my life...*

*To my wife, Elaine,
who has supported me
in my quest to write for the glory of God...*

*To my daughter, Christina,
who has shown me the beauty of creation...*

*And to God,
who has given me life.*

THE BIBLE

The word "Bible" literally means "Book." It actually contains scores of "books" which are numbered differently within various religious traditions. The Bible is read and cherished by those of the Jewish, Christian, and Muslim faiths. This is almost sixty percent of the world. Within these groups, there is disagreement on how the Scriptures are inspired by God. Some believe that the inspiration is as if God were writing the words, while others may hold that the inspiration of the Bible is similar to the way God inspires us today. The Bible was compiled in the Jewish and Christian traditions from approximately 1,500 B.C. to 150 A.D., and has had a profound effect upon Western culture and philosophy.

THE OLD TESTAMENT

The Old Testament was written in the languages of Hebrew, Aramaic, and Greek. The word "Testament" means "covenant" or "contract." This is the major theme of the old Testament: that God will be the leader of the Jewish Nation, and that they will obey his commands. The Old Testament consists of four sections: (1) Law, (2) History, (3) Wisdom, (4) Prophets.

1. LAW (Also known as Torah, which means Law, or *Pentateuch*, i.e., "Five.")
   Genesis
   Exodus
   Leviticus
   Numbers
   Deuteronomy

2. HISTORY
   Joshua

Judges
Ruth
I Samuel
II Samuel
I Kings
II Kings
I Chronicles
II Chronicles
Ezra
Nehemiah
Esther

3. WISDOM
Job
Psalms
Proverbs
Ecclesiastes
Song of Songs

4. PROPHETS
Isaiah
Jeremiah
Lamentations

Ezekiel
Daniel
Hosea
Joel
Amos
Obadiah
Jonah
Micah
Nahum
Habakkuk
Zephaniah
Haggai
Zechariah
Malachi

THE APOCRYPHA
(These books are not accepted by all religious traditions.)
I Esdras
II Esdras
Tobit
Judith
Additions to the Book of Esther

Wisdom of Solomon

Ecclesiasticus

Baruch

The Letter of Jeremiah

The Prayer of Azariah
    and the Song of the Three Young Men

Susanna

Bel and the Dragon

The Prayer of Manasseh

The First Book of Maccabees

II Maccabees

III Maccabees

IV Maccabees

Psalm 151

Scholars differ on the authorship of each of the books within the Bible. Our purpose is to inform you of the content, so we will not deal with origins or authorship. Dates used in this book are traditional.

Opposite: The Fifth Day of Creation
from The Nuremberg Chronicle

LAW

The Book of Genesis

CREATION

T he word "Genesis" comes from the Hebrew
word *Bereshith* which means "in the beginning." It is no accident that this profound

title would later be the label for the study of "genetics." Our "beginnings" are of profound importance, and the Book of Genesis begins with the Creation. This book tells us of God's creation of this magnificent universe from the origins of chaos.

Each "day" brought something special:

1) Light
2) Sky and water
3) Land and vegetation
4) Sun, moon and stars
5) Fish and birds
6) Animals and humans
7) God rested

The time set aside for God to rest—that is, for the worship of God—became known as the "Sabbath," which means "rest" or "cease." In Biblical numerology, "six" became an evil number because it was associated with the idea of a life without worship on the "seventh" day, or Sabbath.

ADAM AND EVE FALL INTO SIN

This story is a profound study of human nature. The Devil, represented as a Serpent, came to Eve

14

in the Garden of Eden to tempt her into disobeying God by eating the fruit that would help her to obtain knowledge of good and evil. He told her that she would not die—even if she disobeyed God—but that she would be a god. Eve was tempted, ate the fruit (an apple traditionally, because in Latin the word for "apple" sounds like the word for "evil"), and then gave it to Adam, who had been silent during her time of crisis. Suddenly they were cast into strong feelings of desire and guilt, and they ran from God. The Lord confronted them, but neither would accept responsibility. God's punishment for all of humanity is that we will live in pain, with struggle, and then we will die. They were cast out of Eden, which means "delight," never to return.

CAIN AND ABEL

The two sons of Adam and Eve worshipped the Lord, but it seemed that the faith of Cain was weak. He was angry at Abel's stronger belief, and killed him out of jealousy. God then asked Cain, who was hiding after the murder, where his brother could be found. Cain replied "Am I my brother's keeper?"

15

God cast Cain out of the community to be a wanderer with "the mark of Cain" on his forehead so that Cain would not be killed by those seeking vengeance.

Cain kills Abel

NOAH AND THE FLOOD

The world became so evil after many years that God told a righteous man named Noah that He was going to destroy all He had made. He instructed Noah to build an ark 450 feet long, 75 feet wide, and 45 feet high, and to bring his sons, Ham, Japheth, and Shem, their wives, his wife, and the male and female of all land animals. It rained 40 days and 40 nights, and eventually the ark landed on Mount Ararat. God sent a rainbow as a sign of the covenant that he would never again destroy the earth through flood.

16

THE SIN OF NOAH

Noah later drank too much wine, got drunk, and lay naked in his tent. His son Ham saw his nakedness and this incident was the origin of the cursed people of Canaan. Japheth and Shem were blessed because they covered the nakedness of Noah. "Shem" is the origin of the term "Semite." Shem was the ancestor of all the sons of "Eber" (Hebrew).

THE TOWER OF BABEL

The world was once again finding an evil heart. The people were so great in their own eyes that they thought they could be as God. They began to build a tower so they could reach heaven, but God stopped this delusion by confusing their languages. Their words sounded like babbling. Human beings were not only evil now—they also could not communicate.

THE CALL OF ABRAM/ABRAHAM
(Approximately 2,100 B.C.)

God called the man Abram from his homeland to move to another land so that God could begin a Holy Nation of the Jewish People. He promised that He would bless "Abram," which means "Exalted Father," to be the father of a great nation, and that He would curse those who did not believe in this Promise.

The Adventures of Abraham

Eventually God changed "Abram" to "Abraham," which means "Father of Many," because he would be known as the father of the Jewish Nation. Abraham had a relative named Lot who was always getting into trouble. Lot lived in Sodom, a place filled with evil. God eventually destroyed Sodom, and Lot's wife died because she could not move forward with her life. Abraham was not perfect either. He traveled to Egypt with his beautiful wife Sarah, and lied about the fact that he was married to her for fear of his life. Basically, however, he was a man of tremendous devotion. On one occasion he met a priest named Melchizedek, who blessed him greatly as he recognized his righteousness. God promised Abraham that his wife Sarah would have a child, and Abraham and his wife laughed because she was much too old. So Abraham had a child with his servant Hagar, and named this child Ishmael. Sarah was jealous, and Hagar and Ishmael fled into the desert. Ishmael is the origin of the people of Islam, according to Muslim theology. Finally Sarah did have a child and God named the child "Isaac" which means "laughter." God ordained as His covenant with his people that every male should be circumcised on the eighth day of life. This day is known in Jewish tradition as the "Bris."

One of the most moving scenes in the life of Abraham is when God tested him by asking him to sacrifice Isaac on a mountain. Just as he was about to sacrifice his son, an angel of the Lord stopped him. He had passed the test of faith. Sarah died, and Abraham bartered with some men to buy land for her grave sight. The tradition of bargaining originated here.

Before Abraham died, Isaac had already met Rebekah. Rebekah gave birth to twins named Jacob and Esau. Jacob was younger—quiet and domestic, while Esau was a hunter—hairy and stupid! Jacob tricked Esau out of the advantageous birthright by

Jacob's dream of the ladder to heaven

wearing a hairy animal skin to fool the nearly blind Isaac into blessing him instead of Esau. Jacob became the man for whom the Jewish Nation would be named. For God gave Jacob the name "Israel" which means "struggles with God." This was based on the powerful story of his wrestling with God—and losing! Jacob also had the famous dream of oneness with God called "Jacob's Ladder."

THE TWELVE TRIBES

Through the relationship of Jacob with Rachel and Leah—whose cynical father-in-law made Jacob work for the love and marriage of his daughters—we received the famous 12 sons or tribes of the Jewish Nation. The sons were as follows: Simeon, Levi, Judah, Zebulun, Issachar, Dan, Gad, Asher, Naphtali, Benjamin, Joseph and Reuben. "Judah" is the origin of the expression "Jewish." Jacob became a wealthy man—and the Holy Nation prospered.

JOSEPH AND HIS BROTHERS

Joseph was especially loved by Jacob, and received a coat of many colors from him. He dreamed that he would rule over his brothers, and told them so! They reacted with anger and sold him into slavery—telling Jacob that he had been killed. He ended up in Egypt as an assistant to Potiphar, but was imprisoned when Potiphar's wife falsely cried rape. Through his ability to interpret the dreams of the Pharoah, he worked his way up to immense power once more. There was famine in the land, but Egypt had followed Joseph's advice and had been saving grain for some time. In a twist of irony, Joseph's brothers came to him asking for food. Eventually the brothers were reunited, and the tribes moved to Egypt. All was well.

The Book of Exodus

THE BIRTH OF MOSES
(1526 B.C.)

All was not well. The empire of Egypt had a new Pharoah who resented the prosperity of the Jewish Nation, and he enslaved them. They were slaves for over 400 years. Moses was born during this tragic period in their history. The situation was so horrible that midwives were instructed to kill male babies so that the Jewish Nation would not get too powerful. The mother of Moses put him in a basket and sent him down the river just after he was born. Pharoah's daughter eventually discovered and raised the child as her own. When Moses was a man, he saw the oppression of the Hebrews, and he killed a taskmaster who was beating a Hebrew slave. Moses went into isolation because he now feared for his own life.

THE CONVERSION OF MOSES

Moses saw a burning bush and went to investigate. He found that it was God. God commanded Moses

22

to be the leader of the Jewish Nation by releasing the Jewish people from bondage to the Egyptians. Moses reluctantly agreed, and was told the name of God. The name was YHWH, which means "I am who I am, I will be who I will be." This name is also written as "Jehovah" or JHVH.

MOSES STANDS UP TO PHAROAH

Moses warned the Pharoah that if he did not release the Jewish Nation then, they would receive signs of God's anger. Pharoah's heart was hardened and he did not respond. God worked through Moses then to produce the Ten Plagues:

1) All water turned to blood.
2) Frogs overtook Egypt.
3) Gnats overtook Egypt.
4) Flies overtook Egypt.
5) Plague on Livestock.
6) Boils on people and animals.
7) Hailstorm.
8) Locusts.
9) Darkness for three days.
10) The Passover.

Moses sends a plague of locusts.

THE PASSOVER

The Jewish Passover orignated in the Pharoah's destruction of the firstborn of every home which did not cover its doors with blood. Pharoah finally gave in to Moses' words: "Let my people go!" The Passover became a yearly ritual celebrating the fact that God delivered his people from bondage.

THE EXODUS

In 1446 B.C. more than 2,000,000 people of the Jewish Nation left for freedom. Pharoah changed his mind, and in anger began to search for them. He nearly cornered them on the shores of the Red Sea, but God parted the sea so the Jewish people could cross while Pharoah's army stood paralyzed behind a miraculous pillar of fire. Pharoah's army was destroyed when they were drowned crossing the sea.

LIFE IN THE WILDERNESS
AS A NEW PEOPLE IN FREEDOM

God sustained the "Children of Israel" in the wilderness through "manna from heaven," a kind of bread that God gave them. He also gave them water through a spring in a rock which Moses found with his staff (a precursor to the divining rod). Moses went to Mount Sinai and received instructions from God—especially the Ten Commandments: (Traditions number them differently, so they are stated without numbers.)

> I am the Lord your God. You shall have
> no other gods before me, you shall not
> make for yourself an idol, you shall not
> misuse the name of the Lord your God.
> Remember the Sabbath day by keeping
> it holy. Honor your father and your

mother. You shall not murder, you shall
not commit adultery, you shall not steal,
you shall not bear false witness against
your neighbor, you shall not covet your
neighbor's house, nor his wife, nor his
servants, nor his animals. (Exodus 20)

When Moses had received all that he needed
from God on Mount Sinai, he went down to the
Israelites and found that they had made a golden
calf idol and were worshipping it. He threw the
stone tablets of the Law of God at them and many

Moses receives the Tablets

died in a terrible earthquake. He called them a "stiff-necked people" and demanded total dedication to the Covenant to obey the Law of God.

THE TABERNACLE

Moses instructed the people to build various temples and equipment for worship such as the incense altar, the bronze altar, the lampstand, and the ark of the covenant. The ark of the covenant was to be the throne of God, signifying his presence. The altar was used for the ritual sacrifice of animals to bring forgiveness of sins. The animal was taking the death that we all deserved, the theology states.

The Book of Leviticus

This word comes from the son of Jacob named "Levi." His tribe was set apart to be priests for the Nation of Israel. Aaron, the brother of Moses, was a leader of the Levites. This book describes different procedures for ritual sacrifice and offerings which seek God's forgiveness and symbolize devotion. Included in the sacred priestly chest were the "Urim and Thummim" which were sacred lots or dice that revealed the will of God. All one had to do was to throw them after a question was asked of God—and they gave an answer. There are also many health restrictions concerning spread of disease, dietary laws for "kosher," i.e., clean food, and instructions for observance of the Sabbath. One of the most holy of days is "Yom Kippur" or "The Day of Atonement." This is when the sins of all are to be forgiven through sacrifice of the scapegoat. Another significant celebration is that of the "Year of Jubilee." This is when all debts are forgiven and all people receive liberty.

The Book of Numbers

The Jews were a people in the wilderness with a religion, but in a rough world they needed an army. This book begins by counting all the men: 603,550. It then records certain religious rituals of this time. For example, it describes the Nazarite, who could neither drink wine nor cut his hair, and who lived in religious devotion. Another section is the famous blessing from Aaron:

The Lord bless you and keep you. The Lord make His face shine upon you and be gracious unto you. The Lord look upon you with favor, and give you peace." (Numbers 6:24-26).

This book also shows that all was not well with the Israelites. They complained because they were tired of eating manna, so they were given quail. Miriam and Aaron began to rebel against Moses at one point, and the surrounding foreign tribes were intimidating. In one situation the people complained against God so frantically that he sent poisonous snakes to kill them. Moses put a bronze snake on a pole, according to the instructions of God, and the people were healed. This came to symbolize medicine.

The Israelites did begin a military campaign to expand their territory, and a king named Balak was afraid of their power. Balak asked a man named Balaam to curse the Jewish Nation, but Balaam could not because he saw that they were blessed by God. This book also tells us of the "Cities of Refuge."

These were places people could go for safety if they were pursued by someone seeking revenge. The idea of "refugee" or "sanctuary" stems from these origins.

The Book of Deuteronomy

Deuteronomy means "repetition of the Law." Here Moses attempted to explain clearly what the Jewish Nation is to believe and do. The central core of belief is found in Deuteronomy 6:4-9:

> Hear, O Israel: The Lord our God, the Lord is one. Love the Lord your God with all your heart, and with all your soul, and with all your strength. These commandments that I give you today are to be upon your hearts. Impress them on your children. Talk about them when you sit at home and when you walk along the road, when you lie down and when you get up. Tie them

as symbols on your hands, and bind
them on your foreheads. Write them
on the doorframes of your houses and
on your gates.

Some Orthodox Jews wear a pathillin—a
leather box with these verses around their arm
(strength), heart (will), and head (mind).

At the end of this book we read of the death of
Moses. God took Moses to the mountaintop to
show him the Promised Land. He would not get
there, but he saw it. This passage was quoted by Dr.
Martin Luther King in his famous "I have a dream"
speech. Moses died and the entire Jewish Nation
grieved.

HISTORY
The Book of Joshua

"Joshua" is the Hebrew word for the Greek name "Jesus." Joshua was given authority by Moses to take the Israelites into the Promised Land, a land flowing with milk and honey. God's call to Joshua was that he "should be strong and of great courage." This book is very difficult to read because of the incredible amount of violence. It is filled with stories of military conquest in which God ordered many of the villages to be utterly destroyed.

RAHAB

A woman named Rahab was an aid in helping the Jewish Nation destroy Jericho. She was later saved from death when the Jews rightly did not harm her during the battle.

CROSSING THE JORDAN
Joshua led his people into the Promised Land. They crossed the Jordan river miraculously, and in a scene similar to the Red Sea Exodus, the Israelites entered into new territory.

JERICHO FALLS
In a ritual involving trumpets and marching, the seemingly invincible city of Jericho saw its walls tumble and its city destroyed by the Jewish Nation.

ACHAN'S SIN
During a battle, a man named Achan stole some of the treasures of the defeated city. He hid them, and the Lord punished the entire Jewish community for the sin of one man. Achan was killed for this transgression, and the Jewish Nation was renewed in its military strength.

MANY BATTLES
The Jewish Nation conquered many tribes and nations in their battles. In one particular battle that they were winning, they asked God to keep the sun out so they could attain victory. This miracle would

be later debated by Copernicus and Galileo—as they rightly insisted that the earth revolves around the sun. Joshua ends by describing the allotment to each tribe of the lands conquered.

The Book of Judges

(Approximately 1150 B.C.)

After the death of Joshua the Jewish Nation needed leaders. The problem during this period of history was that "everyone did what was right in his own eyes." Deborah, Ehud, and Gideon were prominent judges. The most famous Judge was Samson. This was a man who never drank wine or had his hair cut. He was a man of great strength, able to destroy entire armies with "the jawbone of an ass." The section where Delilah tempted him into revealing his power has been the source of many romantic films. He finally got his head shaved, lost his strength, was blinded and was put into slavery. Eventually he regained his strength and destroyed an entire coliseum of mockers by pushing down the pillars holding up the stadium.

This book in general finds the Jewish Nation straying from its roots and without direction.

The Book of Ruth

This is the tragic story of a widow who went with her mother-in-law through devotion to family. Ruth said: "Where you go I will go, and where you stay I will stay. Your people will be my people, and your God, my God. Where you die, I will die—and there will I be buried." (Ruth 1:16). Ruth eventually met a man named Boaz, married him and became the great-grandmother of King David.

The Book of I Samuel

(Approximately 1070 B.C.)

The prophet Samuel was born and dedicated to a priestly life under a man named Eli. This was a time of great unbelief. Even the ark of the covenant was lost to the Philistines for a time. The people thought that they needed a leader; they did not understand that God was to be their Lord. The prophet Samuel annointed a king named

Saul. Saul was a good leader at first, but seemed to have some type of demonic depression or paranoia, and many people lost faith in him. God instructed Samuel to annoint another king named David. After he was annointed with oil, David braved the battle with Goliath by piercing him with a rock. The famous David vs. Goliath—or underdog vs. dynasty—legend began from this incident. Goliath had been a giant of battle, but was slain by a young and meek David. Saul was very jealous of David's popularity and of his relationship with Jonathan, who was Saul's own son. David and Jonathan were best of friends, and this seemed to make Saul insane to the point of attempting to kill David. David fled from Saul's army but showed Saul that he did not want a feud by sparing his life in one instance— and then once more! Saul became so obsessed that he summoned a spiritualist from Endor to bring the spirit of Samuel back to life for his instruction. Saul's life ended tragically in a losing battle as he fell on his own sword—taking his life.

The Book of II Samuel

The death of Saul eventually healed the division within the Jewish Nation and it began to prosper as a great empire. The ark of the covenant was brought to Jerusalem—for now it was David's city—a holy city of the people. King David was caught in a horrible scandal in which he impregnated a married woman named Bathsheba. After many acts of deception he had her husband killed by assigning him to the front lines in battle. The prophet Nathan confronted David about this with a poignant story about a man who lost the only ewe lamb he had to a rich man. David was horrified by the injustice of the story, and then was told that this was exactly what he had done. David asked for forgiveness, but Nathan told him that his punishment would be the death of his son. It was so. Another scandal involved a son of David named Amnon and his daughter Tamar. This brother raped his own sister, and Absalom killed Amnon. Absalom, another son of David, was driven from the land, and rebelled

against his father, King David. Absalom would later be killed by the military when his hair became tangled in the branches of a tree. David grieved with

King David composing the Psalms

passion for the death of his rebellious son. Years later David would be known as a brilliant writer of songs and would die the leader of a great nation. He left his son Solomon to gain the crown.

The Book of I Kings

(Approximately 950 B.C.)

Solomon was asked by God to request anything that he wished to have and it would be given to him. Solomon asked for wisdom. God was so amazed at the request that he granted wisdom and all material things that would follow. The most famous story of his wisdom is of the two women who were arguing over custody of a child. During the night, one woman had found that her child was dead, so she switched the dead child with a live one. Solomon did not know whom to believe, so he ordered the child to be split in two so that they could both have the child. The real mother said "Don't kill him." Solomon gave the child to the one who cared for its life.

Solomon also built a temple and a palace, and lived in a lavish lifestyle with a thousand women at his convenience. The ark of the covenant was brought to the temple in Jerusalem, and the Jewish Nation was now one of the greatest empires of the world. The Queen of Sheba came to visit Solomon because she heard of his great wisdom.

But all was not well with Solomon. He had many wives who turned his heart away from God, and rebellions began to spring up against him. He died, and all of the new kings were disastrously weak, with but a few exceptions. The Holy Nation, created to be a light to the world, began to live in darkness.

ELIJAH AND ELISHA

During these apostate years, God sent prophets to tell the people that if they turned from God, He would turn from them. The most famous work of Elijah took place on Mount Carmel, where he told his people that they must decide whether to follow the true God or to worship false idols. God rained fire for Elijah, and everyone saw that his God was God. Elijah also confronted the evil king Ahab and his wife Jezebel for killing the man Naboth for his vineyard. He was blunt and certainly not a coward to confront the king of the Holy Nation. Elijah never tasted death, for he was taken to heaven in a whirlwind. This was witnessed by Elisha, according to II Kings.

The Book of II Kings

The prophet Elisha was now a witness in the nation that was turning away from God. He performed many miracles, such as helping a widow with sustenance and bringing a son back to life. Except for a few kings such as Hezekiah and Josiah, the leaders of the Jewish Nation brought destruction to the land. By 586 B.C. the entire Holy Nation was destroyed and in slavery. They had nothing. They were in bondage to the Babylonian Empire. They had lost this great empire because of their unbelief.

The Books of I and II Chronicles

These books simply try to "chronicle" the events described earlier through dating, geneologies, and clarification of facts.

The Book of Ezra

(540 B.C.)

This book shows that there was hope. God worked through the Persian King Cyrus to restore the exiles of the Holy Nation to their land and to rebuild the Temple which was destroyed. Ezra prayed for his people, and they confessed to the sins of apostasy.

41

The Book of Nehemiah

Nehemiah looked over the rebuilding of the wall of Jerusalem and of the city itself. Once again there was hope, because the people were prayerful and contrite.

The Book of Esther

Esther became Queen under King Xerxes. She asked the king to confront a man named Haman who had a plan to destroy all Jewish people. She had the courage to confront the king because of a man named Mordecai who persuaded her to follow her compassion for her people. Haman was eventually hanged, and Mordecai was celebrated as a hero because he stopped a plot to kill the King and the Jewish people. The Jewish festival of Purim is celebrated from this book.

THE WISDOM
LITERATURE

The Book of Job

Job was a righteous man who seemed to have everything. Satan asked God if Job would believe in Him if all that he had were taken away. Satan was allowed to bring disaster to Job's life, and Job spent much time with questions

God speaks to Job, by William Blake.

and pain while three friends tried to help him. This is the source of the phrase "patience of Job." In the end, Job asked God this question: What is the meaning of human suffering? Certainly this is one of the main questions of life! God's answer was a question: Did you create the Universe? In essence, God was saying that we could never understand this subject while we live here today.

The Book of Psalms

The word "Psalms" simply means "songs of praise." Many of these were written by King David, and they are written to music which we no longer understand. The Psalms can point us to God, argue with God, and inspire us to live for God. The most famous Psalm is the twenty-third: "The Lord is my Shepherd." Psalm 22 begins: "My God, My God, why have you forsaken me?" This verse was quoted by Jesus on the cross a thousand years after it was written.

The Book of Proverbs

Many of these sayings were written by King Solomon. The most common are as follows: "'The fear of the Lord is the beginning of wisdom," (1:7); "He who brings trouble on his family will inherit the wind," (11:29) (used for the title of the play about the Scopes Trial); and "Pride goes before the fall," (16:18). The Proverbs are written as little "philosophies" in everyday life.

The Book of Ecclesiastes

The word "ecclesiastes" means "preacher" or "teacher." This is probably the most powerful book in the Bible for modernity because it talks about the meaninglessness of life without knowledge of God. The writer, who tradition suggests is Solomon, began the book by crying "meaningless, meaningless." He then called life a "chasing after the wind." The most famous passage is found in Chapter Three:

There is a time for everything and a season for every purpose under the heaven. A time to be born and a time to die, a time to plant and a time to uproot. A time to kill and a time to heal, a time to tear down and a time to build. A time to weep and a time to laugh, a time to mourn and a time to dance. A time to scatter stones and a time to gather them, a time to embrace and a time to refrain. A time to search and time to give up, a time to keep and a time to throw away. A time to tear and a time to mend, a time to be silent and a time to speak. A time to love and a time to hate, a time for war, and a time for peace."

No matter what Solomon acquired in life—sex, money, power, etc.—he could not seem to find peace. Maybe he was showing us what life was without God, or with God but in a fallen world; or maybe he had lost his faith.

The Book of Song of Songs

This book, along with the Book of Esther, which didn't mention God, was almost not accepted into the Bible. It is too romantic for most theologians. It is filled with love letters from Solomon and to Solomon. A few popular phrases from this book are: "His banner over me is love," and "Love is as strong as death." Some theologians regard this book as an allegory about the relationship between God and the faithful. It certainly celebrates love!

THE PROPHETS

The prophetic books were written by men who lived through the history of the Holy Nation. They are not in chronological order.

The Book of Isaiah

The name "Isaiah" means "The Lord saves." Isaiah was a prophet who lived during the destruction of Israel. He warned King Ahaz that the Holy Nation would fall if its people did not obey the covenant. He also comforted the people by telling them that one day the Nation would be restored. Famous quotations from Isaiah include: "Though your sins are like scarlet, they shall be white as snow,"(1:18); "They will beat their swords into plowshares," (2:4); "Holy, Holy, Holy, is the

Lord God Almighty," (6:3); "The Lord will give you a sign: a virgin will give birth to a son, and he will be called Immanuel," (7:14); "The wolf will lie down with the lamb," (11:6); "A voice of one calling in the desert: prepare the way of the Lord!" (39:3); "They will soar on wings like eagles; they will run and not grow weary," (40:31); "By his wounds, we are healed," (53:5).

The Book of Jeremiah

The name "Jeremiah" means "The Lord exalts, establishes, or throws." All of these things were done to this young prophet as God impelled him to speak to the Holy Nation prophetically. He is known as the weeping prophet; in fact, the word "jeremiad" means a long lamentation. He lived to see the destruction of Jerusalem, and much of his ministry consisted of warning the people that they would be destroyed if they did not change their lives and way of worshiping the Lord. One of the kings enjoyed burning Jeremiah's writings in public.

49

Jeremiah loved to use illustrations. One illustration he used was the story of the the linen belt that was buried, and therefore ruined. The belt symbolized the Holy Nation, which had buried its head in pride and was now in ruin. Jeremiah also likened human beings to clay and God to the potter. He thought that this is the most perfect life: to be molded by God each and every day. The most famous verse for Christians is in Chapter 31, in which Jeremiah speaks of a "new covenant" in which the love of the Lord will be in all people's hearts.

The Book of Lamentations

Jeremiah was the author of this book. The word "Lamentations" literally means "How?" This book questions human suffering, asks why we hurt one another, and wonders if Israel's bondage to the nation of Babylon will ever end. One of the most shocking sections of this book tells of a time of starvation in which children were eaten by their parents. In the midst of this lament, however, God tells us that there is hope.

The Book of Ezekiel

The name "Ezekiel" means "God strengthens." Ezekiel needed the strength of God because he lived during the time of the destruction of Jerusalem. When his wife died, he was told not to mourn, just as he should not mourn at the destruction of the Holy Nation. One of his most famous visions was that of the "dry bones." He saw dry bones take on flesh and life through the power of God's prophecy. This symbol gave hope to the Jewish Nation that their "dry bone" life of slavery would some day end. The song which reads "Leg bone is connected to the ankle bone..." originated from Ezekiel. Ezekiel also described some flying machines early in his book which certain New Age theologians have interpreted as flying saucers!

The Book of Daniel

Daniel had a gift of interpreting God's will and other people's dreams. One vision was of a hand sent by God to write a cryptic message on a wall. The expression "the handwriting is on the wall" comes from this story. In another story, Daniel was caught praying to God and was thrown into a lion's den because he had broken the law. Daniel was not harmed by the hungry lions, and his accusers were thrown into the den and eaten. The main point of this book is that

Daniel, by Peter Paul Reubens.

God is the Supreme Ruler, and that no country truly has control over a people. This is comforting for a people in exile.

The Book of Hosea

The name "Hosea" means "salvation." Before the destruction of the Holy Nation the people were arrogant, materialistic, and promiscuous. God brought judgment on them, according to Hosea, so that they would return to Him and receive salvation. Hosea compared the Holy Nation to an adulterous wife. He named his children "God scatters," "Not loved" and "Not my people." He told his children to fall away from the theology of an adulterous nation and to return to God.

The Book of Joel

The name "Joel" means "YHWH is God." He told his people that the attack of locusts they were experiencing was like God's army attacking their sinfulness. He also declared that the drought was the judgment of God and would continue until the people returned to a more holy life.

53

The Book of Amos

The name "Amos" means "burden." God was going to put a great burden on the properous Holy Nation. Amos preached before the Fall of the Jewish Nation. He saw their immense wealth not shared with others. He witnessed empty worship and vast immorality. He predicted their destruction.

The Book of Obadiah

When all had been lost by the Holy Nation, the Edomite people laughed at the hardships of the Jewish people. Obadiah declared that their laughter would be turned into tears, as a faithful Holy Nation would some day rise again.

The Book of Jonah

In this narrative Jonah was asked to preach to his arch enemies the Assyrians. He refused God and fled to the sea. During a severe storm the depressed Jonah asked to be tossed overboard, whereupon he was swallowed by a big fish. Eventually he was spit out, and he agreed to preach to the Assyrians. They were converted, and he despaired because his enemies would find salvation. God ultimately informed Jonah that true wisdom is service to the Lord.

The Book of Micah

Micah told the Holy Nation that their sinfulness would bring destruction. He was right. But his name means "Who is like the Lord?" This points to the profound forgiveness and grace of God. Micah predicted that the dynasty of King David would be restored through a man born in Bethlehem, (5:2).

The Book of Nahum

The horrible and tortuous reign of the Assyrians over the Holy Nation was ended by God. Nahum means "comfort," because the people were finally released from this terrible bondage.

The Book of Habakkuk

The Book of Habakkuk is a dialogue between the prophet and God. His main question was why God would allow such an evil nation as Babylon to destroy the Holy Nation. God's answer was that ultimately we can never fully understand His plan, and that we should trust in Him.

The Book of Zephaniah

This prophet's emphasis is the Day of the Lord! He predicted the destruction of the Holy Nation, and said that two things would happen to the people—some would be judged, and others would be forgiven.

The Book of Haggai

The name "Haggai" means "festive." King Cyrus of Persia had given permission for the Holy Nation to rebuild the Temple, and in 516 B.C. Haggai spoke at the dedication. Before the dedication he offered encouragement to the people, saying that God would bless them. He told them of the time that a King, a Messiah, would rise and rule over them in glory!

The Book of Zechariah

Much like Haggai, Zechariah was there to give encouragement as the Holy Nation rebuilt the Temple. His name means "YHWH remembers," and he told the people that God was with them. He called for spiritual renewal, and predicted the coming of the Messiah.

The Book of Malachi

Malachi saw weakness in the faith of his people. The people complained that the Temple and the Nation were not as great as they had been under David and Solomon. Malachi means "my messenger," and he prophesied the coming of a messenger who would prepare the way for the Messiah who would bring power and glory.

THE APOCRYPHA

Much of this material was written between the testamental periods. It is not accepted by all traditions as inspired by God.

The Book of I Esdras

This book lists the reforms of the prophet Ezra as the Holy Nation returns to God. It includes a scene of the Passover led by King Josiah and emphasizes a new form and attitude toward worship of the Lord.

The Book of II Esdras

This book was relayed by the angel Uriel and asks how God's love and power could allow such evil in this world. The answer ultimately is that we must trust God.

The Book of Tobit

A righteous man Tobit became blind and was forced to live in the evil city of Ninevah. He was far from Sarah, the woman he loved. Sarah was possessed by demons, and both of their lives were miserable. Their prayers were heard by God, and the Lord sent the angel Raphael to rescue them. God worked through Tobit's son, Tobias, to heal Tobit's blindness and Sarah's demonic possession. Then Tobias and Sarah were married.

The Book of Judith

The general of Nebuchadnezzar's army, Holofernes, surrounded the Jewish city of Bethulia and the people had little hope. Judith seduced the general out of a sense of religious duty and patriotism and then cut off his head after she made him drunk.

Additions to the Book of Esther

These additions to the Old Testament Book of Esther emphasize the religious element in the heroics of Esther. God, who was not mentioned in the original book, is seen as the controlling force of the events.

The Book of the Wisdom of Solomon

This book in a folksy way tells the readers that their lives will end either with God's favor or His wrath. Wisdom is the way to God for the individual and for the Nation as a whole.

The Book of Ecclesiasticus: The Wisdom of Jesus, Son of Sirach

Jesus, Son of Sirach, was apparently a teacher of Jewish wisdom, and in this proverbs-like essay we find much awe of the wisdom of God. An example is "A faithful friend is an elixir of life; and those who fear the Lord will find him," (6:16).

The Book of Baruch

The author of this book was a secretary of the prophet Jeremiah and wrote mainly of the wisdom that comes from God and of the comfort God gives to the fallen Holy Nation.

The Letter of Jeremiah

This letter was written by the prophet Jeremiah to the Jewish people who were taken in exile to Babylon. He told them of the destructiveness of worshipping idols and explained why the people were in such a tragic situation.

The Prayer of Azariah and the Song of the Three Young Men

This is an addition to the Book of Daniel. In that book three Jewish men named Shadrach, Meshach, and Abednego ("Azariah" in Hebrew) were cast into the fiery furnace. Miraculously they were saved, and this prayer and song includes the praise of God for this event.

The Book of Susanna

A beautiful woman named Susanna, which means "lily," was blackmailed by two elders who wished to have sex with her. They threatened to say falsely that she had committed adultery if she refused. She did refuse, and they testified in court that she had been unfaithful. They were about to kill her when Daniel spoke up, showed the contradiction in their stories, and saved her life!

The Book of Bel and the Dragon

A popular idol named Bel in Babylon was given food by the people. The next day it is found that the gifts had been eaten, supposedly by the idol. Daniel found that it was actually the cultish priests who had eaten the food. Daniel also killed a dragon with a potion he had found made of pitch, hair, and fat. He was later thrown to the lions, but returned unharmed.

The Prayer of Manasseh

This evil king of the Holy Nation had been thrown into exile, and he finally prayed in this book to God to ask His forgiveness and to confess to the evil of idolatry.

The Books of I, II, III, IV Maccabees

A man named Judas Maccabeus led many revolts against oppressors to obtain freedom for the Jewish Nation.

Psalm 151

This book consists of a Psalm in addition to the previous 150 in the Old Testament. It is ascribed to King David as he celebrated his victory over the giant Goliath.

THE NEW TESTAMENT

The New Testament was written in Greek, has 27 books and letters (epistles), and dates from the the death of Jesus to the end of the first century A.D. Our dating system is based on the birth date of Jesus Christ. The books of the New Testament are as follows:

Matthew	Ephesians	Hebrews
Mark	Philippians	James
Luke	Colossians	I Peter
John	I Thessalonians	II Peter
Acts	II Thessalonians	I John
Romans	I Timothy	II John
I Corinthians	II Timothy	III John
II Corinthians	Titus	Jude
Galatians	Philemon	Revelation

The Gospels According to Matthew, Mark, Luke and John

For our purposes, we will summarize the Gospels as one unit, although each Gospel portrays Jesus in its own unique way, just as four artists would each paint a portrait differently.

Matthew and John were disciples of Jesus, while Luke and Mark were important figures in the early Church. The Gospels give us brilliant reflections of Jesus.

Mark

JOHN THE BAPTIST

This son of Zechariah and Elizabeth was a cousin of Jesus. He was born six months before the "Lamb of God" to prepare people for Jesus' ministry. He baptized the people as a form of cleansing and repentance, so that they would be ready spiritually for the Son of God. He also foretold of a Baptism of the Holy Spirit and fire which Jesus would bring to the Church. He was later killed by Herod because his voice bothered the conscience of a seductress name Salome.

Salome dances before Herod with the head

The Birth of Jesus

The story of Christmas includes the Virgin Birth, the shepherds, wise men, the manger, and the glory of the angels to God: "Glory to God in the highest, and peace to his people on earth." Christmas brought the Messiah that the prophets had spoken of hundreds of years earlier

JESUS THE HEALER

Much of the ministry of Jesus was spent healing people of their emotional and physical infirmities. His ministry was a glimpse of the restoration of the person in heaven.

JESUS CALLS 12 DISCIPLES

Jesus had "followers and learners," i.e., "disciples." The disciples were: James, John, Andrew, Philip, Bartholomew, Matthew, Thomas, James Ben Alphaeus, Thaddaeus, Simon, Peter and Judas. They all had distinct sins and strengths, but their devotion to Jesus, with one obvious exception, was made even stronger after the resurrection.

JESUS' TEACHING

Jesus taught in parables much of the time. These are allegories which give the listener a vivid understanding of God's wrath and love. Jesus said that knowing God is like a mustard seed (which grows in strength every day), a treasure (which is valuable), a net (which catches fish—and throws away the bad), a merciful servant (who is forgiven, and who should then spread forgiveness), a Prodigal Son (who is lost and then found), a worker (who does not grumble, but knows that the "last will be first"), and a Good Samaritan (who goes out of his way to help people). Jesus also delivered the powerful Sermon on the Mount in which He challenged people to great heights of love in this world. He taught that prayer, humility, and compassion are essential elements in this life, as important as standing firm against sin. This sermon contains the "Beatitudes," such as "Blessed are the meek...," the saying "Judge not, lest ye be judged," and the Lord's Prayer:

> Our Father who art in Heaven, Hallowed be thy Name. Thy Kingdom Come, Thy will be done on earth as it is in Heaven. Give us this day our daily bread, and forgive us our debts, as we forgive our debtors. And lead us not into temptation, but deliver us from the evil (One).

This incredible sermon is in found in Matthew, Chapters 5-7.

Jesus, crowned with thorns, is presented to the crowd, by Albrecht Dürer.

THE RELIGIOUS LEADERS, PALM SUNDAY, MAUNDY THURSDAY, AND GOOD FRIDAY

Jesus seemed to have a great distaste for the relgious leaders of his time. He saw them paying attention to the minute details of the ethical life, while they forgot love. He saw their lifestyles as very hypocritical, and He turned over the tables of the moneychangers that the leaders had tolerated on the steps of the temple.

Jesus entered the Holy City of Jerusalem on the day now called Palm Sunday. The people waved palms and shouted "hosanna" (victory), to their Messiah. Jesus, however, came to change their hearts, and not their political fortunes. This message was not loved by many. Jesus instituted the sacrament of Holy Communion, but when He told them to love God and human beings, they carried out a revolt led by the religious leaders. A decree was issued by Pontius Pilate to have Jesus crucified.

Jesus was killed on the cross on the day now called "Good Friday." Jesus gave His life "as a ransom for many," as He so often said. His sinless life—and His death for an unjust reason—were to take upon Himself the sin of the world, so that all who believe in Him should not perish, but have eternal life. This theology is best summarized in John 3:16.

THE RESURRECTION

On Sunday morning after Jesus had been killed, many witnesses saw him alive. He appeared to his disciples and many other people, and they were inspired to live their lives for Him. Many were martyred for His sake, but found peace in His love and the promise of eternal life.

The Book of Acts

This documentation of the activities of the early Church was written by Luke. The Holy Spirit came to God's Church through a miracle called "tongues of fire" which enabled Christians to communicate the message to people of all languages. Tremendous growth was experienced by this early Church, but persecution was its greatest curse and blessing. The man Stephen became the first martyr for the Church, because he proclaimed his belief in Jesus Christ. One of the enemies of the Church was a man named "Saul," who was converted to Christianity on a journey. He became a great writer and apostle for the Church. He dedicated his life to the mission of spreading the words of Jesus.

The Letter to the Romans

Saul was named "Paul" by God for his new life in Christ. He wrote this letter to the Church in Rome to explain to them that Jesus Christ died so that they might receive salvation. He told them that their works of God were in response to God's love, not to earn his love. They had already received God's love through his grace.

The First Letter to the Corinthians

Paul wrote to this Greek city named Corinth, because its people had philosophical divisions, sexual immorality, and disputes among themselves. He gave a moving essay on love in Chapter 13, and explained that all people should use their gifts from God in love.

The Second Letter to the Corinthians

One of the main reasons for this letter was that many had challenged Paul's apostleship. He defended his right to teach the Word as stemming from his conversion—or God's choice of him—on the road to Damascus.

The Letter to the Galatians

A group of people asked what one mus0t do in accordance with the Law to be a Christian. Paul wrote to these people in Galatia to explain that one does not have to follow Jewish practices to receive salvation. He called them "foolish Galatians."

The Letter to the Ephesians

Paul wrote this letter to the Church of Ephesus to take them back to the grace of God, away from the pagan work ethic that had begun to poison their belief. "Put on the armor of Christ," he said.

The Letter to the Philippians

Paul wrote to this persecuted Church in Philippi to encourage its people and thank them for their faithful witness. He did, however, warn them that while we are free from the Law by the Grace of God, we cannot do just anything we want. One should not cheapen grace.

The Letter to the Colossians

Some believed that you had to eat special foods, punish your body, and have a special knowledge of God to be in His favor. Paul wrote to this Church in Colosse to tell them the error of their ways.

The First Letter to the Thessalonians

These Christians were in the midst of terrible persecution, and Paul wrote them to declare that this world is not all of life. He comforted them with words about God's judgment and the afterlife.

The Second Letter to the Thessalonians

Once again, Paul comforted them during their persecution and told them that the Lord's return would free all from this painful world.

The First Letter to Timothy

Paul wrote to his young church worker to encourage him and to admonish him to resist false teachings. He also instructed him on how to delegate authority in the Church to responsible leaders.

The Second Letter to Timothy

Paul wrote to Timothy as a prisoner, for the apostle felt lonely and depressed. He had been imprisoned for his belief in Jesus Christ under the persecution of Emperor Nero, and he asked Timothy to visit him in prison.

The Letter to Titus

Titus was a convert of Paul's, and he was given authority to work with the Church in Crete. Paul instructed Titus on false teachings, and encouraged him to be strong concerning moral ethics.

The Letter to Philomon

Paul wrote to his friend Philemon on behalf of a run-away slave named Onesimus. He asked Philemon to forgive his slave, and take him back as a brother in Christ.

The Letter to the Hebrews

The unknown author wrote this letter to show that Jesus was a priest from the line of Melchizedek, a man that Abraham had met when he had just been called to begin the Jewish Nation. Jesus is the priest who sacrificed His life for the sins of all people, so that no animal sacrifices need take place any longer.

The Letter of James

James, a relative of Jesus, wrote this letter as a guide for ethical instruction in the Church. He wrote that "faith without works is dead," that we should watch what we say, submit to God, live in gratitude to God, and pray earnestly.

The First Letter of Peter

The disciple wrote that the Gospel was "Good News," and that even in difficult times we should trust in the love of God.

The Second Letter of Peter

Peter told the faithful Christians that they were to remain engaged in the teachings of Jesus—to study them—so that they would know what is false and what is true.

The First Letter of John

The disciple John wrote this famous letter to fight against a teaching called "Gnosticism," which taught that the body was evil and must be tortured. He taught clearly that "God is love," and that all false teachings must be resisted.

The Second Letter of John

There were false missionaries who were taking advantage of faithful Christians. John warned the faithful of these intruders.

The Third Letter of John

John praised a helper of the missionaries named Gaius. He condemned those who did not want to spread the Word of God.

The Letter of Jude

This letter teaches that the freedom of the Gospel does not mean that we can do anything we want. There are ethical standards, not just forgiveness for any sinful lifestyle.

The Book of Revelation

This cryptic book was written by the disciple John when he was in exile. It contains numerous messages about God's plan for history, but the plan is interpreted in such strange ways that it is almost incomprehensible. The book begins with letters to the seven Churches admonishing them for their sins and encouraging them for their strengths. It then opens the seven seals—White Horse, Red Horse, Black Horse, Pale Horse, Prayer that Judgment Day would come, Description of End Times, and Silence. These all seem to indicate a war between the Church and the world. This war is fought with the grace and moral abolutes of God versus unbelief. Death and tragedy enter the world in incredible numbers, and the mark of the leader of immorality is 666—a totalitarian evil number. Ultimately, God will reign—and evil will be destroyed. In perfection with God there is no pain or tears, but eternal love.